Mara Thelling

An Artistic Life
Embrace the Truth Within You

Poems, Prose & Reflections

Copyright © 2021 by Mara Thelling
English Translation Copyright © 2022 by Leanne Cvetan

Originally published in German in 2021 as
Künstler sein: Aus dir entsteht die Wirklichkeit.
Translated from the German by Leanne Cvetan
Cover design: Mara Thelling

ISBN: 9798824837728
Imprint: Independently published

All rights reserved.
No part of this work may be reproduced or transmitted in any form or by any means, electronic or mechanical, including photocopying, recording, or any information storage and retrieval system, without the express written permission of the author.

Mara Thelling
Girardet Haus
Königsallee 27
40212 Düsseldorf

www.marathelling.com
info@marathelling.com

Table of Contents

INTRODUCTION
1. JADE
2. ULTRAMARINE
3. CINNABAR
4. SLATE
5. GOLD
6. TITANIUM

For Lisa, Martha & Paul

INTRODUCTION

I will devote myself to art
I will become
What art desires of me
Free, independent, satisfied
Yet proud and haughty
Toward those who disparage it
And lovingly gentle
To
Myself

Mara Thelling

1. JADE

Before you can find
Art,
You must find yourself.

Mara Thelling

Exquisite, poignant, and somber,
Uniquely designed,
What the future has in store for us.
It is a dream,
A phantasy, a vision of eternity,
Destiny and hope in one.
Infinite, finite, and yet symbolic.
Beguilingly, I can recall
Everything that is still to come.

Mara Thelling

Everything that you paint
And everything that was ever painted in this world,
Existed once before in other dimensions and worlds,
Or still exists.
You are called to be the artist,
To let these thoughts, feelings, intuitions, and even memories
Flow through you,
So that you understand what they are really trying to tell you.
That you are the vessel, through which words, images, and emotions
Can flow out into this world.
And others will look to you
To hear the stories that did and those that still do exist.
All these creatures who tell you their stories
(in your imagination and in your thoughts)
Are there to help you better understand the universe,
To make it a better place.
That is your calling,
Artist!

Mara Thelling

I will stop wanting to be someone other
Than who I am.
I will stop expecting things
And I will discipline myself,
Starting now,
In receiving.
And I shall receive
Joy,
Love,
Goodness
and
Art,
And you,
My soul's beloved.

Mara Thelling

Feeling
Art
Is simply wonderful.

Making
Art
Is even more wonderful.

But BEING
Art
Is the greatest of all.

I am art. You are art. We are art.
We are artists.

Mara Thelling

Artist,
You are not alone!
There are many others like you!
Connect with them!

Mara Thelling

There are works of art, music, literature…
That result from activity, or as I like to say,
Handcrafted.
And there are hidden, cognitive images,
dreams, visions…
Seeking their way into the physical,
Into the worldly presence
They so desire.
For me,
It is more rewarding
To give life to the imagination,
Than to imitate what already exists.

Mara Thelling

Your soul in pain
Covered it in water
And a coating of liniment
Until the pain subsides
And you can feel your heart.
A cocoon surrounds you,
One of kindness and deceit.
One that you alone can decern.
And once your soul is soothed,
Your pain will also subside.
And when that happens, you must ask yourself,
What your soul was trying to tell you in the shadows of the night.
Now that you are glad it's all over.
Indeed, the deepest of pain shall pass,
When your heart starts to love again.

Mara Thelling

The FORMULA for ART

#1

Art is not simply something
that flows through me.

The Universe – Spiritual Energy – ME – Art

Mara Thelling

#2

Art is something that can only arise from
within me
(from my inner self)
and pass through me completely.

ME – Spiritual Energy – Art

Mara Thelling

#3

And then there is art
That emerges from interaction with YOU.

YOU (Spiritual Energy) – ME (Spiritual Energy) –
ME (Spiritual Energy) – YOU (Spiritual Energy) – Art

I am a part of the whole and of creation / of the universe.
You are a part of the whole / of the universe.

Art is the expression of my essence and my spiritual power.
Art is the depiction of all reality or of all imaginable power.

Mara Thelling

Feelings and emotions

Concealed deep within you

Indiscernible

And yet tangible

Your life

Unwritten

You decide

And you see

Something still seen today

Could be hidden behind its memory tomorrow

Buried deep

Safeguard your thoughts

And remember

All that was and all that

Could be true

When you were with me

For ever

In a dream

Mara Thelling

Art is in you and around you.
Reality is what you make of it.

Mara Thelling

I'm going out into nature today,
To restore
My energy
To soothe
My soul
And
To delight
My heart.

Mara Thelling

Deep inside the earth live
Many exquisite beings.
In the darkness and far from any human fuss
They toil.
We humans do not know of their existence
Yet they are there.
And for years,
They resent us humans,
Because we unknowingly are destroying their habitat.
As we equally destroy our own.
Their resentment is an attempt
To warn us
And when that doesn't do the trick,
They will harness the power of nature
To express their desire for peace.
There is still time for us
To decide
To leave on our own
And to leave behind,
That which does not belong to us.
Nature is powerful
And it longs for unity
And to return to a time,
When paradise ruled the earth
And we mortals
Lived in harmony
With life and nature.

Mara Thelling

The window open, I revel in the fresh air
That fills my lungs.
I am overwhelmed,
Overtired.
Unable to think even one clear thought.
What remains?
What is there?
What is yet to be experienced?
I don't know anymore.
The ground under my feet is lost.
Inconsistently consistently, I feel free
When I am idle,
When I sit quietly and watch
How time passes.
But it can't go on forever.
And yet, I need this idleness right now,
This sitting quietly,
To preserve my innermost self.
I am no longer ME.
And until I have found MYSELF,
I will pause,
Mediate,
Rest,
In order to continue again,
To write again,
To paint again.

Mara Thelling

Do not be afraid to attract attention,
For you attract attention in other ways.
Do not be afraid to rest somewhere,
For you won't rest any longer than you need to.
Do not be afraid to leave,
For you won't leave without saying goodbye.
You always stay in the place
Where you are loved,
Where you are welcome,
Where love resides.
Above all, do not be afraid of yourself!
You will proudly be who you are and always have been
Even as you concealed yourself
In all those years of loneliness.
Show your talents to all those
Who mocked you,
Who couldn't fathom,
How it would be one day,
When you grew into yourself.
Determined and free,
You will forge your way from now on.
And you will never again be afraid
Of being seen.
What was once unseeable,
Inconceivable for those
Without the ability to dream,
Is conceivable to you.
You are now visible to all those
Who are able to see,
And they will be your friends.

Mara Thelling

Woman in green

Born in green am I,
Lavishly wreathed
In beauty and pleasure.
I occupy a space,
That honors me
And that gives me hope,
That everything
Will come true.

Mara Thelling

If I open my innermost to the outside
And I reveal myself to you and the world,
What do I have left?

Mara Thelling

When I think today of everything
That happened yesterday,
Sadness sets in.
But still I continue!

Mara Thelling

Your inner artist will
Choose the right colors.

Mara Thelling

2. ULTRAMARINE

I don't have to understand you
Nor you me.
But we need to show respect for one another,
As you would like
To be treated yourself.
And if you take this to heart,
We will have everlasting peace.

Mara Thelling

When fear holds you captive,
Grips your heart and threatens
To swallow you whole,
Do not hesitate to embrace it and tell it
That it doesn't need to be afraid,
That it will be loved until the end of its days
And that there is hope for all those who desire it.

When fear envelops you,
Takes away your sun,
Turns your day into night,
Holds you captive in a tower of darkness,
Light a candle of love
And surround yourself with joy and beauty,
With peace and security.

Then the storm that rages through your soul
Will end.
It will dissipate, like every storm dissipates.
For every storm dissipates.

Remind yourself of things that only your heart can feel,
Of the love and warmth of another time
And show your fear
Love, because it's there to protect you.
Turn away from those who foster fear
For they use it to exact control,
To make us do things otherwise unthinkable without fear.
Love and feel the light in your heart,
It's telling you everything will be fine,
As long as you believe in yourself.
And should you ever lose faith, then come to me.
I will give you a rose that will help you
Be yourself again.
Mara Thelling

I am wary
When actors say
What they themselves think and feel.
What would happen
If then musicians and writers,
Every poet and thinker,
Every laborer and scientist,
Every person on earth,
Said what needs to be said.
If they felt and thought again,
And thoughtfully felt
What is to be seen.
What would happen
If ART united,
Beauty,
Freedom,
And common ground?

Mara Thelling

Art for a year

Try it out
Define new rules
Dissolve rules
Slow down
Create art
Awaken art
Love art
Support art
Find art
Live art

Painting, poetry, music, photography…
Or open a gallery
Install installations
Unite the arts
Art unites

Mara Thelling

Chaos atop chaos
Creates new order.

Mara Thelling

Blue thoughts feel at home
In blue minds.
And blue minds
Reside in freedom.

Mara Thelling

A person is not allowed in this world to simply
BE an artist
No, a person must BECOME an artist
A person needs to LEARN art
And will all this learning comes the emptiness
The monotony
The hopelessness
A person simply IS an artist
There's no need for a certificate
That says
Now you are good enough to create art
For creating art is but a mistake
BEING art
Is
The true calling
Feeling art and
Living art
Is REAL ART.

Mara Thelling

Sometimes it takes years to understand something.
And then overnight,
The next moment,
Unexpectedly,
You take that next step.

Mara Thelling

Give me an answer to all my questions,
Even if you don't yet know
What all I want to know,
You always know everything
Before I can say it,
Before I can even think it,
Before I even feel a thought forming.
Let me be a part of the wisdom of the ages
Of eternity
Of creation
I don't want to leave this world before I have understood it all,
All the unanswered questions engraved in my mind,
All the thoughts that long to be stilled,
All the divine cognizance,
That I can perceive,
But not understand.
Please help me to see,
Why I am ME
And you YOU.
Please help me to comprehend,
What is comprehendible.
Please help me to build a bridge,
From the wisdom of the ages,
Spanning the knowledge of the past,
To all that is yet to come.
I can see it
But not understand it
I need to act
And transform myself
To be with you
For ever
(I love you forever... You know that)
Mara Thelling

3. CINNABAR

No university in the world
Can make you
Into an artist.
Because you already are one!
You only need to look inside yourself
And unlock the art that resides in you.

Mara Thelling

Yes, there are people
Who will understand you
and love
you.
You just have to find them...

Mara Thelling

Love!
I have no method,
For success.
It is all fate, chance, fabrication, or passion.
They are all within me,
But I can't find the key
To the door
That will open them all and still let me be me.
There is no path for us,
For we each go alone,
Even when we only go together.
We embrace.
We kiss.
We make love.
And still the uncertainty remains that we are not one hundred percent ONE with each other,
Wholly loved, protected, embraced.
There is no one hundred percent.
And yet, everything you give me,
And everything I give you,
Is more than I have ever given to anyone anywhere at any time.
I am bound to you, as closely
As could be,
For if it could be any more,
I would dissolve into you
And you would cease to exist.

Mara Thelling

It only makes you stronger,
living in a world
that doesn't appreciate
Art and creativity.
But why should you desire to be strong?
Seek out a home for yourself,
one that your heart likes,
and where you can be weak.

Mara Thelling

Why could you take the paths,
That I never saw
And never would have taken,
If you weren't with me?
Why did I chose doors
That weren't meant for me
And still they opened?
Why did I stop,
To ask you
If you'd stay tonight,
After the darkness smothers the candlelight?
Why was I afraid to tell you
What I really feel for you?
Why did you leave
When I looked at you so urgently?
Why is everything
Now lying at my feet like this?
Why are you there
And I here
And the future has lost its soul?
Why couldn't I hold on to you,
Not let you go,
Not love you,
The way you would have wanted?
Why did our love disappear
Like the starling on its southward flight?
I will wait for you,
For the starling to return next spring.
I will be there,
When you call me and want to make me happy.
I will be there,
To pick up where we left off,
To tell you that I never want to be without you,
And still there were
so many years without you.

Mara Thelling

It is incredible to see
Things that seem invisible.
It is incredible to fathom
What currently drives you.
It is incredible to feel your love,
For I never could have imagined
How it was really is to be with you,
How it could be for ever,
How you love me.

Mara Thelling

I look into your eyes with love
We are one
Grown of the same reed
Our leaves identical
And yet unique
I envelop you
Until our love bears fruit

Mara Thelling

The end has come
To a wonderful time
Of love
And the self-deception
That everything can last forever
There is a sorrow deep within me
And I miss the respite of the refuge
Of lying in your arms
I was happy then

Mara Thelling

Why do you still appear in my dreams?
Because I still love you!

Mara Thelling

My soul restores with you
Energy attracts energy
And thus, your power attracts mines
Nothing can stop me
With you showing me the way
Nothing can come between us
And I disappear in your manifesting light
I let go, to find myself anew
Here and now and for eternity

Mara Thelling

Waste no time on things,
That do not come from your heart.

Mara Thelling

My soul thirsts for you
How plainly I remember
Having loved you
And how truly I wish
To be near you
Not knowing that you would never dare
But my soul longs for you
I see you wandering the dark garden
The moon covered by a foggy veil
I remember you
My love
But today, since the moon shines as bright as day
I can send you my love
And tell you that you don't have to do anything on your own
For every day, every hour, every second I think about
How it is when you are near me
And we walk through the garden together
Holding hands
And whispering into each other's ear
You are mine
And I shall be the same
Think of me on a clear starry night
That the moon has turned to day
And I will think of you

Mara Thelling

How can it be that artists always paint the same thing?
Use the same technique,
Pursue the same motif,
Have the same colors fill the page…
No longer does it spring forth from an inner font,
But is born of outside influences.
It's good to have found one's medium
And it's good, to paint from the heart.

Mara Thelling

4. SLATE

I simply can't find a way.
There is simply no door,
That I can pass through.
Perhaps I am already there,
Where I
Am supposed to be?
Or do I need
To keep searching?
Looking?
Going?

Mara Thelling

Every rule that has ever been set up regarding art,
should be forgotten,
Every color wheel and color theory,
Every musical shackle on your soul,
Every powerless element of infinity,
Because they only stand in the way of expressing your innermost images.

Mara Thelling

Art
Is dead
It has been robbed of its existence,
Not only
Because artists no longer paint, play, write, or make music.
No, but because
It was also they themselves
Who failed
To bring attention to their circumstance.
But even if they
Had done,
What some
Did do,
It is then alarming
That there were so few.
And that so many
Kept silent
About
What was happening to art,
And about
What was happening to the artists.
What is an artist?
And what is art?

Mara Thelling

Real art doesn't exist (anymore)
It is all only handiwork,
Disguised as ART.

Mara Thelling

Yesterday I met an old school friend
again
Is it shocking how some people
Don't change
And do not express any awareness or creativity
In their lives
They are unmotivated and cold
There are people, who are so
Caught up in their own lives
And still, they don't notice it themselves

Mara Thelling

M. shall be immediately
Deleted from my telephone book!

Mara Thelling

I look at
Your face
And your face
Bears sadness.
And this sadness
Is the air in this room
Of people,
Who have given up on
Speaking to one another.

Mara Thelling

Effective immediately, the ART police are on patrol
And if you even think of the wrong image
You will be taken into custody
And repeatedly be told
What images you may think

Mara Thelling

The critics live
these days
primarily
on the balcony!

Mara Thelling

I am fearful
That my words will no longer be understood.
That I will accidently use words
That aren't allowed to be used anymore now.
But there are words today that are (often) unused
Like freedom
Like love
Like art
How times change…

Mara Thelling

Art today is very limited…
Or has it always been?
Everyone bows down to the market.

Mara Thelling

There's no point anymore
In saying anything,
In trying anything,
In thinking anything,
Only to then abandon it.

There's no point anymore
In doing something, or not,
The others will anyway
Still
(For whatever reason)
Hate you.

Mara Thelling

Actors
Are people who perform words
Written by
Others.
But where are the people
Who write those words?
They've disappeared.
Have they disappeared?
And does that then mean
There will soon be no more actors
With anything to perform?

Mara Thelling

If what
Is art to me
Can no longer be expressed
And the grotesque faces of ignorance
And the mob
Win the overhand,
Then this piece of history will
Repeat itself
When it shouldn't have been permitted
to happen in the first place.
But this thing that repeats itself
Is so deeply ingrained in your soul
That it hurts
To watch you die
ART

Mara Thelling

Art & Truth

It takes my breath away
To see the way you suffer
Art / Truth
For your suffering
Is obvious
And in your misery
The hope also dies
That anything will change
And yet, it is so important
Because that
Which you say
Is art / is truth
And because it is
art / truth
It cannot be art /true
And because it is art /true
art / truth
hurts
And because it is art / true
My soul is sad
To see the way you suffer
art / truth.

Mara Thelling

I sing for all the
Artists
Who no longer feel safe
In this realm
To express their opinion
But who have an opinion
In this realm
In this time

Mara Thelling

It is art!
You will not understand it
Can not
Want not
Instead, you
Can
Want
To infer
How good it feels to you
Needs to feel good
Not that it reflects the truth
Or does it?
Exactly the truth
YOU take from it

Mara Thelling

5. GOLD

Complete
Bathed in sparse light
Swathed in gilded hues
I see you before me
A shadow hides your face
And I can only guess who you are today
Long ago I could see
When you smiled and showed me your white teeth, full of joy
It doesn't matter that you've aged, for me, you shall remain the most beautiful being on this earth
But I forgot to tell you that age is fleeting and you shall dwell in youthfulness forever
The one thing that I envy you for today is not your youth or your beauty,
It is the freedom with which you, here in this world, can see
What is both beautiful and macabre in one.

Come to me, for it is such bliss
To you love you here,
As I once did before.
To love you here gives me strength for
thousands of years
And when we truly meet again,
You will have hardly aged and I will be a
young man, to whom you will say,
How wonderful it is that you are here
But wait! You remind me of someone...
Of the...
The one I used to love.

Mara Thelling

Every artistic expression from you
Is
Unparalleled
And
Stands outside
All subjective evaluation
Yes!
It is not even permitted to be judged by others.

Mara Thelling

My skin feels
Your warmth, which I gratefully accept
And feel though you are far away from me
But your radiance will still warm hearts in
thousands of years from now
Even after I am long forgotten
You will still be here
To say to those who follow after me
That is worthy to dwell in your light
For it is complete
Pure
And perfect
Just like you

Mara Thelling

Tell me your secret
The secrets
The formula that makes up your being
Tell me about everything
That only you can see

Don't tell me about
Superficial niceties
Or things you can possess
Tell me about things of grandeur
That can only be understood by the soul
And perceived
By the heart

Tell me the answers to my questions
And I understand
If you don't want to give them to me
Because the answers that one does not seek for oneself
Mean nothing to you
And are insignificant
And still you fail to understand,
That I am looking for YOU

Mara Thelling

6. TITANIUM

I am visible in my invisibility
And still, I hide from you
Out of fear of being rejected
Because you are important to me,
It is important to me
What you think

Mara Thelling

Being
Not being
Being everything
Being real
Being
Being nothing
Having been nothing
Not wanting to have been
Taking no responsibility
Fault
Guilty
Not guilty
Faultless
Being
Is
It
Not
So that
You are
Not the
Way
You
Should be
Since
You are
Who
You should be
But that is not you

Mara Thelling

I don't want constant
interact
With someone or something.
I simply want to
BE!

Mara Thelling

Time and inspiration
Are the artist's allies
Haste and strife
The artist's foes

Mara Thelling

It is terrible to witness
Things repeating themselves
Yet the power that lies in repetition
Is endlessly greater and stronger
Than a new beginning

Mara Thelling

Where do I find you
Where do I find myself
How can it be that we are entwined
But cannot find each other
How can it be
That I sense your voice
That I seek your purpose
How can it be
That you try to find me
And I AM here
On my own
Without you
I do not miss you
For I do not know
That you really exist

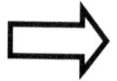

And an illusion tells me
That it will never again be
How it once was
For without you, everything is sunny and clear
Sunlessly foggy
Without you ... I cannot find myself
And without you, I do not know who I really am
And without knowing who I am, who I COULD be
If we ever found ourselves finally
In the future or in the past
Or at any time
We will find truths in being together
No longer alone
Will I be and sometime
You will be near me

Mara Thelling

Being thrown back on your own resources
Devoid of time and space
Lacking of title and means
Lacking status and pleasantries

Being thrown back on your own resources
What remains
What exists
What is allowed?
One's insides turned outward
Thoughts hammering inside your skull
The important things take precedence

Being thrown back on your own resources
Creates a time of intimacy
Creates a time of contemplation
One of reflection
And you understand who you really are
Who you truly want to be
Who you have always been

Being thrown back on your own resources
Selfless in time and realm
Selfless with yourself and others
Selfless in your thought and action
Then you will find yourself

Finally!

Mara Thelling

In the forest is darkness
And light
Here waits something great
For those,
Who await great things
And only those who can see
Will see it.

Mara Thelling

Keep your secrets
To yourself
For at least as long,
As it takes for them,
To find their footing
So as to stand sure
That no slight
attack
From outside
Knocks them down.

Mara Thelling

New Beginning
!
Something comes to an end
Something new begins
Something within me is lost
While time carries on
Something is trying to begin
I don't yet know
where it will lead

There is something inside me
That looks forward to it
There is something inside me
That regrets nothing
That forgives
That is beginning
Something full of hope
It is good
Just as it is

Mara Thelling